M. A Tyler

Egypt, and Other Poems

M. A Tyler

Egypt, and Other Poems

ISBN/EAN: 9783337239930

Printed in Europe, USA, Canada, Australia, Japan

Cover: Foto ©Thomas Meinert / pixelio.de

More available books at **www.hansebooks.com**

AND

OTHER POEMS.

BY
M. A. TYLER.

———

PHILADELPHIA:
J. B. LIPPINCOTT & CO.
1876.

THESE poems were composed from time to time as an amusement for the leisure hours of the writer, and therefore extend through a series of many years. That some of them were written long ago will be evident from the poems themselves.

M. A. T.

PHILADELPHIA, November, 1875.

CONTENTS.

	PAGE
EGYPT	7
THE FUNERAL OF GENERAL FRAZER	13
LINES	16
WASHINGTON'S MONUMENT AT BALTIMORE	17
SONG OF SPRING TO THE FLOWERS	19
STANZAS	21
THE WOUNDED DOVE	22
GOD IS PRESENT EVERYWHERE	23
SEA-SHELLS	25
DRAIN NO MORE THE GOBLET DRY	27
TO THE WINDS	28
MORN AMONG THE MOUNTAINS	31
TO AN INFANT	33
THE ALPINE HORN	34
THE HISTORY OF AN OSTRICH PLUME	36
SONG OF NIGHT	39
THE WILD SWAN	40
HAPPINESS	42
BYRON	43
THE SEASONS	45
PEACE	49
TO C. L. T. IN INFANCY	50

CONTENTS.

STANZAS
SONNET. TO A FRIEND.
INVOCATION. TO L. E. L.
THE ETHIOPIAN LILY IN MY GARDEN.
SEBASTOPOL
HARVEST. A TEMPERANCE SONG.
THE NEW WORLD. A TEMPERANCE SONG
MEMORIAL VERSES:
    IN MEMORY OF HER WHO DEPARTED THIS LIFE SEPTEMBER 17, 1862
    CATHARINE
    TO THE MEMORY OF EMILY
    IN REMEMBRANCE OF A. K.
    IN MEMORY OF H. G. TO HIS MOTHER
    HARRIET.
MAXIMS.

EGYPT

DURING THE GOVERNMENT OF MOHAMMED ALI.

LAND of the Pharaohs and of giant mind,
   What mighty ages have sprung up and stood
A moment poised above thee, then declined
   Into oblivion's pathless solitude!
   Yet leaving grand memorials, that elude
With a tremendous energy the power
   Of man's rapacious fingers, and the flood
Of Time's eternal frettings. Hour by hour
Some beauty has been reft from other artist's dower:

But thou, in thy primeval freshness, seemest,
   In tint and sculpture, but of yesterday,*
And with the wonderful forever teemest;
   For genius here has stamped thy ruins gray
   With quenchless life: and though they've passed away,
Th' illustrious dead, yet still their works of might,
   Which to interpret sages but essay,
Are waymarks on the earth, that tend to light
Creation's record down through a long reign of night.

---

* " Before the gateway of the temple of Luxor, until within a few years, stood two obelisks, each a single block of red granite, more than eighty feet high, covered with sculpture and hieroglyphics fresh as but yesterday from the hands of the sculptor."—STEVENS.

How much of history is there locked within
   The living emblems of thy voiceless tongue!
Ages have passed, and yet men scarce begin
   To trace the characters upon thee flung
     In lavish, strange profusion: 'tis among
Stupendous monuments a nation keeps
   Its self-earned privilege, to live, when hung,
Like thee, with barb'rous shadows darkness heaps
On fallen pomp: alas! no native o'er thee weeps.

Thy headless Memnon and thy trodden shrines,
   Thy sculptured temples falling to decay,
Thy fadeless tints and thousand mystic lines
   Rouse not his soul, for torpor seems to lay
     An icy finger on his soulless clay;
And he whose noble ancestry has made
   A thousand ages but as yesterday,
So fresh, so life-like, are the scenes portrayed,
Has sunk to deepest night: society's last grade.*

Oh! can no ardor rouse him? but to see
   The vast assemblage makes the spirit spring
Up to a higher tone; what majesty
   Thy countless monuments around us fling!
     Thy sons were godlike, and their spirits' wing
Floated through sunnier climes than we behold;
   Their deeds were for the future: lo! they bring

---

* "The Copts are usually regarded as the descendants of the true Egyptians, the subjects of Aminophis and Sesostris. Like all classes of men who have been long degraded, they are remarkable for cunning and duplicity, being a groveling race, and farther distant from civilization than any of their fellow-citizens."

The past to meet the present : strong and bold
Their master-strokes outlive all other works of old.

Is there not still among thy gorgeous tombs,—
   Those structures fitting for their princely dead,—
Some spirit of the past, which restless roams,
   Making all hallowed round the marble bed
   Of this long-mouldering race, whose genius led
Admiring nations to the lore they sought?*
   Is there no sign, amid the ruins spread
In fadeless glory, of the lofty thought
Where inspiration's self the bright conception wrought?

Have they all vanished, body, spirit, too,
   And left no traces save their works behind?
Cannot the fancy find or make a clue
   Wherewith to link us to their lofty mind?
   Grasp the ideal, and with it unbind
The burning thoughts, and make the present seem
   Peopled with airy forms, the light, the wind,
And all things with illusive beings teem,
And the past spring to life as an enchanted dream?

Oh! it is great to blend, though but in thought,
   With beings of such mighty mind and mould,
Who reached afar, and Heaven itself seems brought
   Down from its lofty height.† These men of old,

---

* " Plato, Pythagoras, Lycurgus, Solon, Herodotus, and Tacitus entered into her. (Egypt's) bosom to be initiated into her sciences, religion, and laws."—GLIDDON.

† " In casting my eyes on the ceiling,"—in an Egyptian temple,—" I perceived zodiacs, planetary systems, and celestial hemispheres repre-

With tireless hands of strength and spirit bold,
The Pyramids have reared : with giant might
   They piled them to the sky, where clouds are rolled
Around their summits at a dizzy height,
Stupendous still ! as when they blest Sesostris' sight.

Live on, great Thebes ! * What though the desert sweep
   O'er other cities, be thou still the same ;
Thou wast the cradle, art the couch of sleep,
   Where genius rests : and yet no loftier name
   Stands up against thee with a better claim,
A stronger grasp on immortality.
   Where is the nation that has fixed its aim
So near perfection, or can rival thee ?
Unique must be its life if it undying be.

Proudly, O Nile, thy sacred water glides,
   Gemmed with a coronal of gorgeous fanes :
Thebes, the transcendent, o'er the whole presides ;
   Thy rugged hills are cleft, and on thy plains
   The pomp of kings in silent grandeur reigns.
Temple and tomb and palace, side by side,
   Stand ruined all ; yet Time himself maintains
Deep reverence o'er their dust, as far and wide
And desolate they stand amid their pristine pride.

---

sented. Some of the ceilings are painted blue (as bright now as when first put on, more than three thousand years ago), and dotted with stars."

* " This celebrated city (Thebes) the size of which Homer has characterized with the single expression of the hundred-gated, still impressed the mind with such gigantic phantoms that the whole French army, coming suddenly in sight of the ruins, with one accord stood in amazement, and clapped their hands with delight."

Well have they called thee sacred, lovely Nile!
　　Hast thou not brought the products of thy bed
Deep in the mountain gorge on them to pile
　　Riches no hand, though kingly, could have shed?
　　Hast thou not gently down thy channels led
The oozy waters that o'erstepped the shore,
　　And far their fertilizing tribute spread?
Thy verdant banks prolific harvests bore,
And Plenty filled her horn at the redundant store.

And have not priests and holy hermits blessed
　　Thy precious waves, and brought them to their shrines,
And watched with deep devotion as they pressed
　　Through secret reservoirs in cunning mines,
　　Deep in the temple's cavity,* where shines
No lovely beam from the bright king of day;
　　How have they strewn with lotus-flowers and vines
The placid stream that all unruffled lay,
Sending the odors up from many a floating spray?

The desert, too, came down o'er smiling plains,
　　Drinking whole cities up, and laying waste
Extensive districts, until naught remains
　　Save the broad ocean sands, whose waves make haste
　　To fetch down farther ruin, till are chased
Man, beast, and herbage from their haunts of old;
　　Tombs, labyrinths, are engulfed, whose fronts have faced
The storms of ages, and though sternly bold
They stood defying time, the desert o'er them rolled.

---

* "The supposed tomb (in the great Egyptian Pyramid) was a trough, which, on certain festivals, her priests used to fill with sacred water and lotus-flowers."—WILFORD.

A desolate realm! but not forever so:
    A strange, new fate is thine,—to rise though slain:
The mantle of forgetfulness to throw
    From off thy corpse-like visage: to maintain
    A contest for supremacy again:
To bid defiance to destruction's hand
    That urges on his charioteer amain:
To wake the latent vigor of the land,
And, though it sleep, arise, and with new strength expand.

Thou hast a ruler worthy of the throne
    The Pharaohs honored, despot though he be:
He spake and barb'rous usages have flown;
    He gave the mandate, and at once we see
    Commerce come forth to wed with industry.
A happy union: and their marriage gave
    The land to smile and hold a jubilee.
Where stagnant pools have stood the harvests wave,
The work of him, thy son, the gifted and the brave.

It is enough: thy second spring-time nears;
    Age cannot keep thy powers in longer sleep:
To thee a resurrection morn appears,
    Beams of a dawning light upon thee sweep,
    Scattering the shadows which forever keep
O'er other prostrate realms an endless spell;
    But thou hast wakened from thy slumbers deep;
Unheard-of change: the sapient fail to tell
What thy ulterior fate may be; so fare thee well.

THE FUNERAL OF GENERAL FRAZER.

General Frazer fell on the side of the British during the American Revolution. He was interred at evening in the midst of the engagement. An incessant cannonade was kept up while the chaplain officiated. As soon, however, as the Americans discovered the funeral procession, they ceased hostilities, and, in honor of the gallant commander, fired minute-guns.

THEY mount among the dusky trees,
But leave no trace upon the breeze:
No trampling sound of horse is there
To mutter on the mountain air;
But o'er the plain the cannon's breath
In murderous accents thunders death.

Around them ball and shot are driven
Like rattling showers of hail from heaven:
The sulphur smoke and blast of war
Are rumbling up the mountain far:
As crash of thunderbolt they come
With peal of horn and sound of drum.

The ancient forest hears the sound,
And trembles o'er the quivering ground:
The elm-tree bows its pale green form
In answer to the martial storm;

But naught withholds that phalanx still,
It winds through ravine, mounts o'er hill.

The evening shadows, dusk with glooms,
Settle along their waving plumes;
The pine-trees o'er them hang a screen,
A living veil of fadeless green;
The stars look out, and yet they go,
That little band of silent woe.

They mount still higher: now they rove
Like spectres through the mountain-grove:
Their robes float back upon the breeze,
As slow they wind among the trees;
One effort more, and now they stand
Silent as death, that little band.

All is not hushed: the battle-cry
Rolls its deep surge along the sky;
The seeds of death come leaping free
To reach that spot of misery:
And glance, like thunderbolts of dread,
Around each proud, unyielding head.

They stand like martyr by his tomb,
Dilating in the thickening gloom;
No warlike sound can rouse them now,
Stern sorrow sits upon each brow,
And seems to mock at outward strife,
Scorning alike or death or life.

They move not, for the dead is near;
They quail not, for they know no fear:

They have been nursed in war's embrace,
They have met danger face to face;
They have stood forth upon the field
Where armies fell and empires reeled;

But never have they known before,
In battle din or wild uproar,
A feeling of such quenchless power
As gathers in this bitter hour;
It is not grief alone they bear,—
Indignant thoughts are burning there.

Their lips are curled, but every eye
Turns to the earth all reverently.
Now sudden bursts upon the ear
A death-dirge, slow and deep and clear:
A union sad of martial strain
With solemn chant for hero slain.

But, hark! the battle din is o'er,
The clarion's breath is heard no more;
The minute-gun alone is there
To break the stillness of the air;
The strife hath ceased: the foe hath said,
"Bury in peace your honored dead."

LINES.

Lady, with a step so nice,
Hast thou ever weighed the price
Of the fur robes round thee flung?
Think'st thou of the tortures wrung
From the feeble tribes they blessed
Ere they folded o'er thy breast?
Lovely are they, and how warm,
Pressing softly round thy form;
But remember! for thy pride
Has been poured the life-blood's tide:
Pangs, unwaken'd by offence,
Have been wrung from innocence.
Oh! within the peaceful shade
Havoc, havoc hath been made!
Blood has poured like rain for thee
From the veins of purity.
Would that beauteous fur could bear
Tokens of the deep despair,
When the gory knife has pressed
Quivering in the victim's breast!
Would it could depict the woe
When the snare has laid him low,
And the blood through mouth and ears
Started like a flood of tears!
Then thy heart would yearn with grief,
And humanely prompt relief:

Aid would render in such hour;
Pause! for much is in thy power.
    Should not woman's voice be heard
Wheresoe'er the air is stirred
With the blighting things that spread
Under Cruelty's broad tread?
Rouse, then! teach the world to see
Mercy has its germ in *thee*.

WASHINGTON'S MONUMENT AT BALTIMORE.

MONUMENT of him who stood
Where the fiery battle flood
Mingled with the gory blood:
    Speakest thou of victory?

Or of conquering chief, who came
Onward like a rolling flame,
Glory's halo round his name,
    Circling broad and brilliantly?

Reared in peace for deeds of war,
Up the steep of Time afar,
Tell his name where ages are,
    In the dark futurity.

And amid the storms that bear,
From their lofty mountain lair,

Mighty oaks on cars of air,
    Lift thy brow triumphantly.

Statue, on the summit high,
Touching neither earth nor sky,
Realms may waste, and sink and die,
    Thou, too, fall ingloriously.

Babylon its pomp has seen,
Silence broods where Troy has been,
Spoiled are courts of Egypt's queen,
    Hushed is Balbec's revelry.

Thus thy shaft may fall away:
But the *name* shall not decay;
Time, with his full trump, shall say,
    Washington eternally!

SONG OF SPRING TO THE FLOWERS.

    Come from your wintry beds,
My beautiful and lovely; flowrets gay,
    Come from the pillow where you laid your heads
When Boreas, in his fur-car, passed this way;
    Come from your wintry beds.

    The turf is warmed for you:
For I have brought the sunbeams in my train;
    Silent and bland they force a passage through
The cold and sullen soil, till fresh again
    The turf is warmed for you.

    Come from the meadows gay:
I have been o'er them, and prepared the sod;
    Come, that with gentle pressure I may lay
Benignly on you the blest beams of God;
    Come from the meadows gay.

    Come from the prairies vast,
Where I am present with my wooing heat;
    Come, with your regal glories unsurpassed;
Send up your odors as an incense sweet;
    Come from the prairies vast.

    Come from the mountain-side,—
Old Winter has dealt roughly there, I ween,—

Yet come with double strength and triple pride;
Rear thick your tufted heads the moss between;
   Come from the mountain-side.

   Come from the forests deep:
Lift the leaf-covering from each shrinking face;
   Come, while I lure you from your wintry sleep
In the dark foldings of the earth's embrace;
   Come from the forests deep.

   Come from your wintry beds,
My beautiful and lovely; flowrets gay,
   Come from the pillow where you laid your heads
When Boreas, in his fur-car, passed this way;
   Come from your wintry beds.

STANZAS.

There are before thee gem-like flowers,
That sparkle in the summer bowers;
Above thee, and from pole to pole,
Orbs of resplendent glory roll.

The air around thee glows with song,
As the gay warblers dart along;
Light, scent, and sound appeal to thee,
To raise thy soul in sympathy.

Then leave the dull, perplexing cares,
The tread-mill round thy life that wears;
Look up! there's something more below
Than pressing toil and grinding woe.

What if thy life be cast in gloom?
Smile, and the rose of hope shall bloom.
All is not lost when darkness lowers:
Sure, sunlight follows after showers.

Others have been where thou art now;
Then cheer thee, smooth that troubled brow:
The darkest hours precede the day;
Be hopeful: clouds shall pass away.

THE WOUNDED DOVE,

FOUND IN THE WOODS BY THE WRITER.

Though the heavens are high and wide,
Yet a shaft is in thy side.
Wherefore wouldst thou flee in fear?
Nay, the fowler is not here.
I will screen thee from his eye,
Should he now be lurking nigh.
Flutter not; my hand may bring
Comfort to thy wounded wing.
Ah! thy silver hue is dyed
With the fountain from thy side:
And the moss beneath thee bends
Where the trickling gore descends.
I would staunch the blood with care,
And would smooth thy plumage fair.
But thine eye of light is blind,
And thy pinion droops behind.
Could I but thy powers restore,
I would ask for thee no more;
But would say, Go, mount on high,
Take thy pathway near the sky;
Float upon the upper breeze;
Rest but in the loftiest trees;
Make thy nest sublimely proud,
Where the hemlock sweeps the cloud.

When thy music swells with love,
Pour it to the heavens above;
Come not near the earth again,
Minstrel of a plaintive strain.

GOD IS PRESENT EVERYWHERE.

In the cloister, in the shrine,
　In the temple's solemn gloom,
In the deeply buried mine,
　In the chambers of the tomb,
In the flood and in the air,—
God is present everywhere.

Countless leaves and untold flowers
　Speak Jehovah, mute, but plain.
Are not all the vocal bowers
　Choirs for earth's extended fane?
Heaven and earth His impress bear,—
God is present everywhere.

He is in the ocean's roar,
　He is in the wild-wood shades,
Where the rills forever pour
　Music through their lone arcades;
He whose glory none may share,
God,—is present everywhere.

GOD IS PRESENT EVERYWHERE.

In the lightning flashing by,
   In the songster's mellow lay,
In the purple arch on high,
   In the zephyr's rustling play,
Do not many tones declare
God is present everywhere?

Cavilers, in your hearts He made
   Altars meet whereon to lay
Offerings, to His mercy paid.
   Turn not in your pride away!
Doubt ye that *His* eye is there?
God is present everywhere.

In the busy haunts of life,
   In the midst of pleasure's throng,
In the battle's fearful strife,
   In the dance and in the song,
Your vain thoughts His glance shall bare,—
God is present everywhere.

Sufferer on the bed of pain,
   Prisoner in the dungeon's gloom,
Wanderer on the faithless main,
   Pilgrim to the peopled tomb,
Bow the knee in fervent prayer,—
God is present everywhere.

Wearied one, no longer grieve:
   Rise from earth, thy smiles relume;

Hope for thee again shall live,—
    Live in trust beyond the tomb.
Banish from thy heart despair,—
God is present everywhere.

SEA-SHELLS.

The men that trod the earth when lay
    These petty things beneath the sea,
Where are they? Passed, all passed away,
    Brief as the mist upon the lea;
While your wan bosoms, countless years,
Were washed by Ocean's briny tears.

When the young Earth was fresh in pride,
    And Pleasure's bowers no serpent feared,
But fair as bright and blooming bride
    Her virgin innocence appeared,
Then they were cradled by the wave,
Or nestled in some ocean cave.

Far down among the coral bowers,
    Where finny wings glide noiseless by,
They slept through Ocean's wildest hours,
    Calm 'neath their crystal canopy;
The tangled seaweed o'er them spread
Lay like a mantle on the dead.

The sea, the heavy surging sea,
   The sailor-sexton of the brave,
That tolls in wild sublimity
   A death-dirge o'er its empire grave,
Hath, with an artist's magic spell,
Burnished each tiny citadel,

And brought them forth, a lovely boon,
   Fair as the lily, Summer's bride,
To glitter in the gay saloon,
   The pageant of a harmless pride:
In wreaths of many flowers to twine,
Pale relics from a watery shrine.

And thus from out the depths of time
   May we arise beyond the grave,
Still purer in the spirit's prime
   Than sea-shells from the ocean-wave,
To be enwreathed among the just,
Where thief is not, nor moth, nor rust!

DRAIN NO MORE THE GOBLET DRY.

Drain no more the goblet dry:
Let the wine-cup shattered lie,
And its deadly venom flow
In a stream of noxious woe;
Sink it deep beneath the clay,
Dash the poisoned bowl away.

Lo! the vine-bough on the wall
Rears its purple coronal:
And the clustering grapes are seen,
Thick, the trellis-work between;
Grasp them, and thy thirst allay:
Dash the poisoned bowl away!

Summer brings a generous freight,
Bushes bowed beneath the weight
Of the clustering fruit that swells
From their leafy citadels.
God has sent them: make them thine,
Cast away the deadly wine!

High upon their lofty stems
Ruby cherries gleam like gems:
Goodly fruits of every hue,
Autumn spreads before thy view;
Taste them, and the wine-cup leave:
Give thy soul a long reprieve!

From the slayer of thy health
Turn unto the orchard's wealth:
It has treasures richly nursed
That will quench thy fever-thirst;
Fly, then, from the reveler's roar:
Rise to manhood's state once more.

TO THE WINDS.

Whence come ye, minstrels? from the sunny plains,
    Where your soft fannings swayed the drooping flower,
Languid for want of unreturning rains,
    And wasting slowly as the precious dower
Of female loveliness, seen for a day,
           Then, mist-like, borne away?

Perchance ye've journeyed o'er the billow's crest,
    That curled on high in many a snowy fold:
Tossing the dolphin from his place of rest,
    And making sport of him; though strong and bold,
He wages puny warfare with the sea
           When ye are loosed and free.

Have ye not rocked the sailor on the deep?
    Hushed him to slumber when his toil was o'er?
Piped your glad voices to his midnight sleep,
    Till all his early dreams came back once more,
And the sad tones that sighed a last farewell
           Seemed in your blast to dwell?

Oh! rock him still! let thoughts of home be blent
    With all the bright illusion slumber brings:
Kind looks return, that so imploring bent
    On his at parting; soothe the grief that wrings
The tear-drops from his eye: pause o'er his sleep;
              A moment let him weep.

'Twill soon be o'er: to-morrow he will rise
    To buffet fierce your strong, resistless power.
When thunder-peals and lightning rend the skies,
    And darkness mantles on the noontide hour,
And your stern pinions hurl the clouds along,
              Then shall his soul be strong.

What have ye met upon the trackless tide
    Besides the sea-boy in his floating home?
The spicy shores where precious perfumes glide,
    A wasted incense o'er the ocean's foam;
Gay, tropic flowers that wave beneath the trees
              In isles of Indian seas.

And brilliant birds amid the orange-bowers,
    With rainbow plumage glittering in the light,
And date-trees waving through long summer hours,
    Burdening the air with sweets: making your flight
Dreamy with odors of the palm and lime
              Of that delicious clime.

But ye have come by strangely devious ways
    From prospects wilder far, and yet as true:
From Hecla's summits, whose volcanic blaze
    Athwart the frosty sky a glory threw;

TO THE WINDS.

Methinks ye braced your wings till they swelled high
   Beneath the polar sky.

And ye have swept Sahara in your flight,
 Heaving the sand-heaps like a billowy sea:
And where the noonday shone, producing night,
 Engulfing deep the desert argosy.
What is returned upon your muttering breath?
   Despair, alas! and death.

Then let me hear you when your tones are gay
 With the glad music of the woodland bowers;
Speak of the fountains as they chime away
 In some wild glen: and bring the breath of flowers
From the lone prairies, where without a tree
   Rolls a vast floral sea.

And send your music-voices, low and sweet,
 To all the weary, suffering sons of men;
Wherever temples throb, or pulses beat,
 Come, as a gentle, soothing benison:
In low, sweet murmurs come, e'en as a hymn
   From guardian cherubim.

MORN AMONG THE MOUNTAINS.

A BROAD, light streak upon the horizon burns,
    And upward mounts among the clouds on high,
Whose edges brighten in successive turns;
    An artist's hand hath touched the glowing sky,—
    A master-touch: the artist, Deity.
Farther and wider streams the golden light,
    The lower clouds blaze out in burning fire:
The quickening influence pierces to the height
    Of heaven's meridian; fast the rays aspire,
    Till morn's resplendent flame forms night's funereal pyre.

The amber light hath reached the mountain's brow,
    In undulating brightness far 'tis spread:
Feeble at first, but gathering splendor now,
    On every peak a glory new is shed.
    The airy warblers from a leafy bed
Come forth with greetings to the opening day:
    While o'er the leaves a golden light extends
As fast they shimmer in the morning ray,
    And wake to life; the breeze its presence lends,
    And all the wavy mass in changeful lustre blends.

Rills from the mountain in a joyous light
    Come, as bright prospects to the heart when young;
And foaming torrents from the dizzy height,

Where giddy summits to the sky have sprung,
  Dash from the rocks, and to the depths are flung.
And o'er the gulf which mocks the plummet's line
  The graceful bow lifts up its airy form,
Touched with the colors of a Hand Divine;
  Begotten of the mist and sunbeams warm,
  It comes, a child of light, to die amid the storm.

Beneath, the river murmurs as it spreads
  Upon the couch of adamantine stone:
Its onward course through many an opening leads
  In mountain passes, to the eye unknown,
  Save of the fallow deer and fox alone.
Upon its breast the cloudy vapors lie
  Above, below, extending far and wide;
The sun hath touched them: lo! they mount on high;
  Slow rolls the huge bulk up the mountain's side,
  Till, lost in air, it spreads into its kindred tide.

TO AN INFANT.

Lovely infant, in thy smile
Sorrow might her pangs beguile.
Sin might gaze and turn away
From the evil thought that lay
Buried in his heart, and be
Better for the sight of thee.
Vanity might check her wiles,
Witnessing thy artless smiles.
May our love for thee not rise
Farther than is good and wise!
Death may come and rend the tie,
Pale the cheek and close the eye;
But we would dispel the fear.
Years to come mayst thou be here
In the world, but free from grief,
Last in sin, in goodness chief!
Strong to battle ills of clay,
Swerving not from wisdom's way!
Dawn of years and prime's full hours,
Age's frail but sacred powers,
All to one grand object tend,—
Faith's fruition, Time's great end.

THE ALPINE HORN.

"When the sun has set, the herdsman who dwells upon the highest habitable spot takes his horn and pronounces audibly and loudly through it, 'Praise the Lord God!' As soon as this sound is heard by the neighboring herdsmen, they take their Alpine horns, and repeat the same words."

    THE rocks and hills have heard
The pealing anthems of the Alpine horn;
To its deep music forests old are stirred,
    As on the breeze 'tis borne.

    From countless cots below
Responsive notes arise in grand refrain;
Wakening the echoes as they onward flow;
    Sublimely wild the strain.

    Hushing the tones of men,
It swells: a melody profoundly deep,
Pealing through glacier-field and icy glen
    Where the wild chamois leap.

    Up the tall peaks it springs:
Blending its chorus with the spheres on high;
From lofty crags the solemn cadence rings
    In deepening symphony.

Swelling, it surges wide
Till all the mountain seems to breathe of prayer ;
And through the gorges rolls, a music-tide
   Borne on the night-winds there.

Glorious the gathered sound :
As if each pinnacle an angel trod,
And poured his worship from the summits round,
   With, " Praise the Lord our God !"

How thrilling and sublime
To hear the voice of praise go up in air,
From temple where the ardent soul must climb
   To lay its incense there !

Such chorus, unsurpassed,
Among God's monuments alone can be :
Stupendous mountains, forests, oceans vast
   Are fanes for Deity.

And here it is, oh, here,
The altar should be made that He can prize ;
There is no *fitting* temple, save such sphere,
   Beneath the wide, blue skies.

THE HISTORY OF AN OSTRICH PLUME.

1860.

I was reared in the desert: the sunbeams that went
To my root in the ostrich exuberance lent;
And the winds of the sand-sea, though fervid with heat,
As they shot through my fibres, were wholesome and sweet.

I grew up apace, and with pride I stood high,
All waving in light as the sun swept the sky;
But short was my glory: my plumage so gay
Caught the eye of a sable one passing that way.

A chase now ensued: "And whatever betide,
It is mine," he exclaimed, "for the locks of my bride."
I waved in the breeze, or I trailed in the sand,
As the sooty foe followed with noose in his hand.

My parent fled onward, not deeming that I
Was the gewgaw pursued with such covetous eye.
She dashed o'er the sand-heaps, the desert's wild thrones,
And scattered the piles of the wayfarers' bones.*

---

* "In Arabia, the bones of dead men and camels are the principal guides of the pilgrims."

Her feet plowed the sand, and her wings clove the blast,
As a storm-driven vessel, on, onward she passed;
For the foe was behind her, and swiftly she fled,
Till the meshes closed round her unfortunate head.

The death-blows came down with a merciless hand:
They plucked me, and left her alone on the sand;
My streamers now floated, all dazzling and white,
O'er a proud ebon beauty of Congo the bright.

And with my soft fringes above her dark brow,
I still might be waving all gracefully now;
But the man-stealer hasted, and fierce on his prey,
Like blood-hound, he bounded, and bore her away.

And loose from her temple unbraided I swung,
As her arms o'er her head in wild gestures were flung;
The turf where I rested was smiling and fair
As the dawn of the morrow,—but she was not there.

I followed her footsteps, and over the sea
They brought me to flaunt in "the land of the free."
"The free?" it is mockery; for bondage is there,
And the slave is bowed down with the weight of his care.

When the young swain of Congo first placed me above
The brow of his beauty, my price was her love;
But gold (how degrading!) must purchase me now,
For the knees of this nation to money-gods bow.

At length I was bartered: and o'er a fair head
My pure, snowy fringes all gracefully spread;

I drooped on her forehead: its paleness but seemed
To deepen in pallor wherever I gleamed.

Alas! for the av'rice that brought me afar
To regions so strange 'neath the lone western star;
And alas! for the maiden of Congo the true,
And her comrades: the victims of avarice too.

Far better that now, both to them and to me,
The tocsin of woe from the "land of the free,"
The nation of "great institutions" alone,
Had still been a summons unheard and unknown.

Farewell, then! for now I am doomed evermore
To a worthless existence on this distant shore;
And she, the dark maiden, what, what is *her* doom?
The taskmaster's mandate, e'en down to the tomb.

SONG OF NIGHT.

I have come, and toil has fled;
    Gently, gently I will lay
Slumber on the aching head,
    And will lull the cares of day.

O'er the pastures I have trod,
    Shadows on my footsteps pressed;
And upon the humid sod
    Weary oxen are at rest.

Softly o'er the hills I go,
    And my tireless vigils keep
Where the flocks, like spotless snow,
    Lowly on the greensward sleep.

Through the forest I have passed,
    Darkness is its covering shield;
And the wounded hare at last
    Has found shelter in the field.

Day had beams too bright for him
    When he laid him down to die,
So I hung my curtain dim
    O'er his filmy, death-like eye.

Thus I scatter mercies round
  As my footsteps onward move,
Hushing every jarring sound
  With a benison of love.

THE WILD SWAN.

The lake is my home, and its billows I plow;
My feet are my oars, and my breast is my prow.
The wind is my car, and my wing is my steed,
And away through the air I am wafted with speed.
On the lucid, still waters I tranquilly float,
As lightly as nautilus wafting his boat;
And the skies in their purity over my head
Their curtains of azure translucently spread;
While the shadows of stars as they lambently burn
Far up through the depths of the waters return.
My wing is unfettered, my pathway as free
As the clouds of the air, or the waves of the sea;
I skim o'er the mountains, unscathed by the peak,
And the cool, gushing fountains delightedly seek.
There, there hath the hunter not ventured to roam,
And my callow brood nestle secure in their home.
O'er their slumbers suspended the vine-blossoms twine,
And their wild cradle-hymn is the moan of the pine.
And sweet is their sleep in the moss and the fern,
When back to the clefts of the rock I return.
On the oaks of the forest, all knotted with age,
The spring-time for centuries has printed a gauge;

And yet to the breezes alone have they stirred,
The boom of the rifle they never have heard.
Then sleep, my young water-fowls, sleep in your nest:
I will shield you at night with the down of my breast;
And when a few mornings have risen anew
O'er the depths of the fountain so glassy and blue,
I will lead you away on its bosom to bound,
And flutter your pinions like snow-flakes around.
Then aloft on the breezes your free wings shall rise,
The valleys beneath you, above you the skies;
Far up from the mountain, the lake, and the stream,
Till like a white speck on the azure you seem.

HAPPINESS.

What art thou but a phantom? I have seen
    The eager crowd pursue thy shadowy ways,
And vainly seek to tread where thou hast been;
    Thine is a gilded pinion: the light rays
Of bursting meteors as they cleave the blue,
      Even as thou, art true.

'Tis so at least in what pertains to these
    Strange labyrinthine scenes, miscallèd home.
Alas for us, that we must cross the seas
    Of death's dark flood, where spirits only roam,
Ere we can hold thee, never more to part,
      Fast to our yearning heart!

BYRON.

What, impassioned son of flame,
Were the gifts that wrought thy fame?
Genius: 'twas resplendent too,
Checkered though with deadly hue;
Eagle-pinioned to ascend,
Downward yet its aim and end.

Wit: to thee it did but bring
Brightness with a venomed sting;
Wielding oft a poisoned dart,
That recoiled upon thy heart;
Blotting glorious things and high
With a pen of Stygian dye.

Love: and vainly did it glow,
Nursing oft an inward woe;
Folded in its flow'ret's bells
Canker-worms had made their cells;
Deeply in the heart to lie,
There to gnaw and never die.

Fancy: which would scarcely be
Trammeled by mortality;
But, like vapor, to the sky,
Fled to find affinity;

And like vapor, still the same,
Back returned from whence it came.

Feeling: *it* a curse but proved,
Weaning those that would have loved;
Chasing with its own unrest
Kindness from another's breast;
Yearning though for happier life,
Subject still to inward strife.

These united, o'er thy head
Halo-like enchantment shed;
Beautiful, but like the fire
Curling from a deadly pyre;
Or as scintillating beams
'Mid a night of hideous dreams.

Splendid gifts they were which brought
Mental threads by thee inwrought
Into tissues, lovely, fair,
Such as poets seldom wear;
But, alas! the cords of sin
With their woof were woven in.

Oh! how sad that gifts like thine,
Gifts so rare, almost divine,
Should be tethered in their birth
To the lowest forms of earth!
But perchance, it may be, thou
Know'st it well, and mourn'st it, *now*.

Therefore let our pity flow
For thy life of splendid woe;
Thankful, since along our way
Snares of genius never lay,
If to us there be but given
Brighter hopes than thine of heaven.

THE SEASONS.

SPRING.

I know thee by the brook set free
From icy chains, the budding tree,
And by the blackbird's voice of glee,
   So joyous in the field.

I know thee by the violet's glow,
And by the sprouting mistletoe;
I know thee by departing snow,
   Creation's wintry shield.

I know thee by the lowing sound
Of distant kine, the lambkin's bound,
And by the freshly-tinted ground
   That like an emerald glows.

I know thee by the murmuring things,
The beetle's hum, the insects' wings,
The honey-bee, whose music-strings
   Are tuned beside the rose.

I know thee by the starting grain,
By April's balmy, sunlit rain,
And by the welcome frog's refrain,
          Which music is to me.

And more, thy lineaments I trace
In gladness on the human face,
Elastic mien, and joyous pace,
          Sweet harbingers of thee!

SUMMER.

I know thee, too, by sunbeams fair,
Which, in the crucibles of air,
The subtle vapor-clouds prepare
          That seem so strangely coiled.

I know thee by each gorgeous dye
That evening pencils on the sky,
Where raptured limners gaze, and sigh
          To find their efforts foiled.

I know thee by the lightning's blaze,
And by the long, long sultry days,
When the fierce sun his fire-brand sways,
          And flocks in thickets hide.

I know thee by the breezeless woods,
The parching fields, the wilting buds,
The arid beds no streamlet floods,
          Where cattle turn aside.

AUTUMN.

Unnumbered are the things that tell
Of thee; and these I know full well:
Not the pale lily's spotless bell,
   Nor yet the cowslip's dye,

But the far-spreading, boundless plain
All tinted o'er with golden grain,
Where Ceres holds prolific reign
   Beneath the genial sky.

Well, well I know thee by the haze,
The dusky sunlight of thy days,
The spiritual thrill that sways
   The soul with torpor bound.

Not like the joy that Spring unbinds,
Not like the fervor Summer finds,
But like that power in human minds
   Which hallows all around.

WINTER.

And thee I know, thou wintry King!
Full oft I've felt thy furious wing
Athwart my shrinking bosom fling
   A shiver deep and drear.

By all thy glittering, icy glow,
Thy landscapes white with dazzling snow,
Thy leafless trees and flow'rets low,
        I know when thou art near.

By piping winds and drizzling rain,
And hailstones dashing on the pane,
I know thy mighty car amain
        Is rushing toward our clime.

Then cease my strain, lest o'er my soul
Its smiting wheels, charged at the Pole,
Should, heedless of the Muses, roll,
        And hush my babbling rhyme.

PEACE.

This world contains no shrine in its wide sphere
For the sweet dove of Peace; its realms appear
Places of sojourn, not as homes of rest
For that half earthly, but yet heavenly guest.
Pleasure has tempted her a few fleet hours
To furl her pinion in the siren bowers;
But, quick on wing, she mounts the distant height
For scenes more pure, 'mid realms of living light.
Religion, too, has tried her power in vain
To keep the wanderer in her blest domain.
She seems to love the charm Religion yields,
And lingers oft amid her balmy fields.
A richer lustre spreads around her bowers,
Diviner odor sprinkles on her flowers;
But yet when storms appear (and storms will rise),
She spreads her downy wing, and cleaves the skies.
Perennial only she, where Virtue's bloom
Is never quenched in death, beyond the tomb.

TO C. L. T. IN INFANCY.

Welcome, sweet babe! the Muse's lay
Has never hailed thy natal day.
Be then these lines the first frail flowers
To greet my Catharine's infant hours.
I would not ask a life for thee,
Although so dear, my child, to me.
But since thou *art* upon the road,
A pilgrim to the home of God,
It is but meet that years should prove
Experience to the hearts we love.
It were but vain to hide the thorn
That, sure as death, with life is born.
Then, loved one, know, before thee lie
Sunshine and shade upon thy sky;
For the heart's phases may be read
In solar ray and tempest dread.
Could now thy little bosom feel
But half the weight of woe and weal
That thrice ten summers may supply
The sorrow or the ecstasy,
Oh! it would heave in wild commotion,
As slender bark upon the ocean.
But weep not; tears should not bedew
Those placid eyes of heaven's own blue.
Sure I might tell of countless things
To rouse thy future fancyings;

I might bring glimpses of life's joy,
Without its probable alloy;
Hope, friendship, love, with all their smiles,
And pleasure's ever varying wiles;
But would it always be thus bright?
Sure, darkness follows on the light;
Yes, in the heart the tares are strown,
And nourished where the wheat was sown.
Throughout thy life 'twill be a toil
To weed the thrice-prolific soil.
Experience tells me thou wilt find
A field of labor in thy mind:
Passions oft checked, but rising still,
Mocking the efforts of the will.
And thou mayst find thy heart to bleed,
The trusted changed, a broken reed.
Oh, then, my child, let life appear
A pathway to a better sphere.
What though that path alternate lead
Through thorny brake and flowery mead,
Regard it all with equal eye,
As nothing to Eternity.

STANZAS.

'Tis sad to feel the spirit's ebb,
  The flame that lit the soul expire;
The meshes rent in fancy's web,
  The light retire.

Oh! thus to know exhaustion's spell
  Sink deep within the bosom's core,
The waters drained from feeling's well,
  The heartstrings wore,

The taper light not in the soul,
  As once it lit in joy's career,
The sundered chord, the broken bowl,
  This, *this* is drear.

Oh, life! what art thou, when are gone
  The lovely visions hope inspires?
Even as meteors mine have shone,
  Consuming fires.

All that is brief is like the flame
  That burned with but too bright a glare;
Time with his wing athwart it came,
  And made it flare.

Another breeze, and it may go,
  Too fleet to last, too frail to rise;

STANZAS.

Its oil is spent, its wick is low,
         Its lustre dies.

And thus my spirit sinks in gloom,
   A lethargy, of all the worst:
A weary blank, a mental tomb
         I cannot burst.

But shall it not beyond the grave
   Rise as the moth, new-fledged and free?
One hope remains, but will it save,
         And even me?

I'll watch and wait: there yet may be
   An anchor to the tossing soul;
In the long future faith may see
         The clouds unroll.

Surely hope's day-star has not set,
   Only is veiled from mortal eye;
But wears its own bright beauty yet
         Beyond the sky.

SONNET.

TO A FRIEND.

Fair were the hours, but, ah! how fleet and fast
   They vanished from my vision, like a dream
All tinted o'er with radiance as they passed!
   How beautiful! 'twas life's glad morning beam.

How have we talked away the hours of night!
   How have we wandered through the greenwood bowers,
Making Time's pinion but too fair and bright,
   Strewing Life's pathway with the heart's fresh flowers!

Oh! these were moments that the soul may prize,
When thought lies clouded 'mid her troubled skies;
These too were seasons that the mind can bless,
And call them happy when the glad heart pours
A tide of joy on some succeeding hours,
Rich with the bosom's purest tenderness.

INVOCATION.

TO L. E. L.

Oh! tell me, thou whom earth-born feelings bound
   In captive chains of ever-burning thought,
Whose life, though soon its heavy coil unwound,
   And rendered back the cruel price it brought,
Was chastened here, we trust, for realms on high,
              What is Futurity?

Speak, and I'll trust thee; for thy soul is free,
   Free from the cumbrous clog, corporeal clay:
Its doubts have vanished, and obscurity
   Fades as a mist before meridian day;
All things are lucid now: though once a cloud
              Pressed on it like a shroud.

What hast thou found amid that far-off sphere?
   Faith, too transcendent for our mortal ken?
Virtue, so beautiful it cannot wear
   An aspect suited to the sons of men?
Beauty, so thrilling that the ravished eye
              Is tranced in ecstasy?

And hast thou 'scaped from sorrow? freed one, say
   Does anguish enter in that broad domain?
For if *it* be heaven's heritage, I'll lay
   My weary head on mother earth again,

And supplicate the clods and stones to keep
                My soul in endless sleep.

Nay; heaven is heaven, and not a place of woe,—
    Hast thou not found it such? I trust thou hast,—
A place of perfect bliss, where pleasure's glow
    Is stamped on all, and shall forever last;
Where all the air in that bright realm above
                Is redolent of love.

And thither, too, at last, I long to come,
    And freely breathe that atmosphere divine;
Amid those blissful bowers to make my home;
    For here, my anxious heart has yearned, like thine,
To find its fondest hopes, its worthiest deeds,
                All, all but broken reeds.

Come to me, then, and lay thy spirit-hand
    Upon my fevered brow, and let me hear
One sentence only from that better land
    Ere I upon its confines vast appear:
Tell me but this, in tones of heavenly love,
                "Sister, there's peace above."

THE ETHIOPIAN LILY

IN MY GARDEN.

TALL through the myrtle leaves it sprung,
    More glossy and more fair;
And o'er the tinted rosebud flung
    A queenly grace and air.

Was it that it had caught the mien
    Of Cleopatra's pride?
When once her glittering barge was seen
    On Cydnus' waves to glide?

Fair courtier hands have grasped its stem,
    Bending beneath her prow,
To grace the sparkling diadem
    Upon her regal brow.

The boatmen of the Nile have been
    Familiar with its grace,
And through a thousand years have seen
    Its fair, ancestral race.

The gallant barges as they passed
    Laid countless blossoms low;
But where its lot at length is cast
    There comes no keel-like foe.

Brightly, amid a sea of green,
   It rears its snowy head,
And cowslips at its foot are seen
   Upon their tufted bed.

Though it has wandered from its bower
   On Egypt's ancient rill,
Strange visions round it seem to shower,
   And vaguely through me thrill.

For in it lie mysterious spells,
   Mute histories round it cling;
Suggestive more than spiral shells
   Where ocean anthems ring.

It tells of times when men of mark
   Dwelt by the Nile's far stream,
And Moses in his bulrush ark
   Smiled 'mid his infant dream.

When Pharaoh in his pride of state
   Trampled the river's bed,
Sealing his own eternal fate
   In vengeance on his head.

It has an utterance that can swell
   E'en here to this far shore,
Where its lone race may proudly dwell
   When mine shall be no more.

SEBASTOPOL.

"The cost of the late war in the Crimea, to England, is now ascertained to have been, in round numbers, eighty million pounds sterling."

ENGLAND groans, and well she may;
Hark ye! she has cast away
In her self-will, reckless, blind,
Wealth that would amaze mankind.

Wherefore were her coffers drained
With a zeal as though it rained
Floods of riches, which have been
Only by Aladdin seen?

Did she with this boundless store
Open nature's secret door?
Foster genius, till its ken
Pierced the latent powers of men;

Make the human soul to see
Hidden things that yet may be?
Girdle earth with railroad belt,
Widen seas, and mountains melt;

Send unuttered words to glide
Underneath the ocean tide,

Till each coral grove and glen
Pulsates with the thoughts of men?

Or for pomp was it alone
Spent in piling brick and stone?
Rearing structures proud to hold
Pigmy lords of mortal mould?

Compassing the earth to hoard
Luxuries for the pampered board?
Fetching dainty things to grace
Evanescent beauty's face?

Not for these things was it given,
Not for these, nor yet for heaven;
Not to send with silvery tone
Peace on earth through every zone.

Not to smooth the brow of care,
Not to breathe the Christ-like prayer;
Sending it as dew among
Every kindred, tribe, and tongue.

Where, then, did her treasure go?
'Twas to purchase human woe;
Lo! it went to rear afar
Monuments to "*glorious*" war!*

---

* " War is utterly and irreconcilably inconsistent with true greatness. Man has worshiped, in military glory, a phantom idol, compared with which the colossal images of ancient Babylon are but toys; and we, in this favored land of freedom, in this blessed day of light, are among the idolaters."—CHARLES SUMNER.

Seek it where your legions lie
Mangled 'neath a Russian sky,
Where the war with savage rule
Blasted, wrecked Sebastopol.*

Mighty nation! proud thou art
With thy giant-pulsing heart,
Whose deep throbs from Britain's shore
Circulate the wide world o'er.

But what art thou? weakly, mild,
Even as a new-born child;
In the moral sense to see
War a deep enormity.

Oh! thou hast some sage ones there;
Listen to their earnest prayer;
Stifle not their warning word,
Prophets are they of the Lord.

Brothers, say they, what is life?
Waken from your dream of strife;
Few and evil are our days,
War is sin in all its ways.

Leave it; and should discord lower,
Settle it by suasive power;
Crush contention in its birth,—
Peace should be the badge of earth.

---

* " For eighteen months the storms of war beat upon the helpless town (Sebastopol), and left it the saddest wreck that ever the sun has looked upon. Not one house escaped unscathed, not one remained habitable, even."

HARVEST.

A TEMPERANCE SONG.

Nursed by sunbeams, dews, and rain,
Lo! the earth is ripe with grain;
Look around! the very sky
Brightens with the amber dye,
As the winds are o'er it rolled,
Like a wavy sea of gold.

See the reapers: forth they pass
O'er the pendent, dewy grass;
Merrily they onward move
Through the meadow, glen, and grove;
Pausing where the wheat is bright
In the morning's rosy light.

Now the sickle strikes the grain;
Onward moves the sturdy wain;
Pond'rous sheaves, a bounteous yield,
Stud the groaning harvest-field;
And the air is stirred with song
As the reapers move along.

Little deem they that their toil,
Lavished on the generous soil,
Shall be blasted: sorrow's train
Rise from out that golden grain:

Sighs be heaved, and tears be shed,
O'er the blessings round them spread.

By a dark, transmuting power
Man has gained in evil hour,
These are blessings which may prove
Anguish to the souls they love;
And this wealth for banquet shed
Turn to curses on their head.

From these gifts *they* see but poured
Treasures for the ample board;
Ignorance is blissful, then,
Happy reapers, on again;
Wield the sickle, chant the lays
To the bounteous Giver's praise.

Seek not to unfold the scroll
Sin has sealed around the soul:
Making man's demoniac will
Pander to th' unhallowed STILL;
Changing gifts of nature's hand
Into blight upon the land.

Dark and dreadful is the strife
Rum has waged with human life;
Darkness broods, an earthly hell,
Where his blear-eyed legions dwell;
Manhood sinks degraded, dead;
Souls lie crushed beneath his tread.

THE NEW WORLD.

A TEMPERANCE SONG.

I have been to her forests, the red man was there;
I have been to her caves, where the wolf has his lair;
I have scaled the high mountains, their apex have seen,
While the vales of rich verdure were laughing between.
And there was no tempter, no poison I found,
For water, bright water, was gushing around.

I saw her again, and the forest lay low;
I beheld the lone wigwam, unstrung was the bow;
I sought for the footprints the bison had made,
But traces were recent of plowshare and spade;
And in the bright valley where beauty was found
Stood the engine of death, a dark demon unbound.

I looked for her altars; the votaries were there,
But an oath was the worship, a curse was the prayer.
The land seemed to mourn, and the beautiful sky
Was dim, as the fumes of the still-house rolled high.
Oh! bosoms were joyous and faces were bright
When water, pure water, was quaffed with delight.

Our scutcheon is tarnished, our nation is dyed
With the streams of the wine-press, pollution's dark tide.
Arise in your valor, ye strong ones, and save
The land from destruction, the drunkard's vile grave;

On, on with your toil, till our country is free
From the bacchanal song of the mad debauchee!

Yes, muster your legions, for just is the strife,
To war for your brethren, their honor and life;
They sink to perdition, unbind the deep spell,
Break, break the strong fetters forged darkly in hell;
Let your watchword be freedom, and temp'rance your goal,
Peal the trumpet of hope to the sin-stricken soul!

MEMORIAL VERSES.

IN MEMORY OF HER WHO DEPARTED THIS LIFE SEPTEMBER 17, 1862.

Thou hast left mourners here, spirit withdrawn,
But, tell me, tell me, whither hast thou gone?
Through night's long vigil I have watched alone,
And yearned to meet thee; but a wall of stone
Seemed reared between thy spirit-life and me;
Where art thou, loved one, 'midst Eternity?

Once, and once only, in my dreams thou came,
And, oh! so like thyself, unchanged, the same.
Clad in thy mortal robes, no cloud to hide,
A real presence standing at my side;
Eyes that have looked on me were on me there,
Replete with mortal life, though but of air.

None else discerned thee; I alone had power,
A gift of sight to see thee in that hour.
Why wast thou veiled from others and unknown?
For yearning hearts were there besides my own.
Strangely mysterious; was the power to see
Fancied or real? was the vision *thee?*

A precious omen (let me hold it fast),
That in some spirit-realm thou'rt safe at last,
And free; yes, free to come and take thy place
On earth among us : present face to face.
And wilt thou do it oft? No voice replies.
Alas! the barrier betwixt earth and skies!

The world seems lonely since the sentence dread,
The solemn utterance reached me, "She is dead!"
No one again will fill thy place to me;
No meetings more save in eternity.
Then let me trust; in patience let me dwell,
Nor feel the words are final,—Fare thee well!

CATHARINE.

For nine-and-twenty years 'twas ours
    To watch thee on thy onward way,
Strewing life's pathway with the flowers
    Of home-born duties day by day.

Oh! had the messenger been stayed
    To some remotely future day!
It was so sad to see thee fade
    Thus early from our sight away.

Hopes clouded that were once so dear,
    Dark auguries of a coming fate
Which clung around thy presence here,
    Now make thy home all desolate.

We miss thee at the noontide hours,
    On porch and lawn beside the door;
We miss thy hand among the flowers,
    We miss thee always, more and more.

But most of all at early night,
    When all familiar ones are there
Around the well-known parlor light,
    We miss thee in thy vacant chair.

All day we seem to watch and wait,
    And fancy thou wilt come again,
Till evening closes long and late
    To find the fond delusion vain.

Thou'lt come no more; and we must be
    (How difficult our will to bend!)
Submissive to the dread decree,
    And wait and trust unto the end.

TO THE MEMORY OF EMILY.

Sleep on, my loved one, nor awake;
   Ev'n could a rustling leaf restore,
I would not on thy slumber break,
Nor from thy bliss one moment take,
   For grief is past and pain is o'er.

But I will picture to my view
   The happy hours we've mingled here,
Precious but short; they ever drew
From me a fond response and true;
   Remembered now but with a tear.

Far, far away thy tomb is made;
   No tear of mine can fall o'er thee;
Oh! that beneath our broad oak shade
Thy form at rest were gently laid,
   And there, mine too, might some time be.

One hope had long my heart possessed,
   To meet again this side the tomb;
But be it thus: 'tis God's behest;
Thou art, I trust, forever blest,
   Transplanted hence in heaven to bloom.

And if the flower just opening here
   Fulfill on high the promise given,

How glorious in that upper sphere
Will be the beauty it shall wear
   Amid the seraphim of heaven !

I once had hoped that we might bear
   Together on life's rugged road
The smiles of joy and frowns of care;
But *thou* hast found a haven where
   To anchor safe ; that haven, God.

Then let me rather seek to raise
   A thankful heart that thou art free ;
That few and brief have been thy days;
And join with thee to hymn His praise
   Who clothed thee with Eternity.

IN REMEMBRANCE OF A. K.

WE met long since; but yet thy smile is there,
   Graved on my memory like a thing of light;
The bright blood flushed thy cheek, the raven hair
   Was parted on thy brow; all warmly bright
Those looks are on me still: their radiant beams
Live in my soul like sweet but mournful dreams.

We had grown up amid familiar things;
   The same bright landscape opened on our sight;
And memory's hallowed power before me brings
   Visions of days too joyous and too bright;
Too bright and joyous, for the tomb appears
To tarnish all with its corroding tears.

Our hearts have bounded with the same wild glee,
   E'en as gay fawns our buoyant spirits sprung;
Blithe as the lark, and as the chamois free,
   Our young, glad voices on the winds were flung.
And this is past; alas! we may not prove
Our youth's young charm refined by time and love.

I cannot see thee as the grave portrays;
   No, thy dark eyes flash out their wonted beams;
And the bright visions of our early days
   Spring up before me, till the present seems
Not what it is,—a saddened scene to me,—
But real life, and brightened still by thee.

IN REMEMBRANCE OF A. K.

I fondly hoped—that hope, alas! how vain!
   As are, indeed, all worldly hope and care—
To burnish yet afresh our friendship's chain,
   And lightly round my heart its fetters wear,
And make the hours to come more brightly green
In feeling's growth, than youth's glad days had been.

But this is now too late; remorseless time
   Has ravished from me what was all too bright;
Wast thou too good, too precious for this clime,
   That thou wast summoned to the realms of light?
Oh! for submission to the dread behest,
A heart to say, the Almighty will is best!

Thou art but sooner gone; I hear the call,
   And must ere long my vesture gird to go;
The shadows of the grave around me fall,
   And the dark waters of oblivion flow
Coldly and sternly round; I hear their boom,
The dirge-like moan, precursor of the tomb.

Farewell: that word pertains alone to time;
   Thou hast not heard it on that far-off shore;
One pang was thine, and then that better clime
   Burst on thy sight, where partings are no more.
I shall lay down my weary burden too,
And yet ere long; till then, dear friend, adieu.

IN MEMORY OF H. G.,

WHO DIED AT THE AGE OF FIFTEEN. INSCRIBED TO HIS MOTHER.

YEAR after year that opening blossom grew
   In rich luxuriance, bright and fair and gay;
O'er the dark days of toil, like gentle dew,
   Its presence shed a freshness on thy way.

When sad and adverse sat life's wayward tide,
   And with its waters sorrow's tears were blent,
Then he, the loved one, faithful at thy side,
   To all thy weary days a radiance lent.

Where is he now? where is the flow'ret's bloom
   That late so brightly decked the vernal bower?
He smiled on life, he vanished to the tomb,
   Leaving but memory of the bright young flower.

But when the tint has left the lovely rose,
   And the charmed eye no more its glory fills,
What odors still its ruined folds disclose!
   And from its depths what sweetness yet distills!

So from his memory shall an incense rise
   Sweeter than perfume from the rose's bed;
And wheresoe'er thy future pathway lies,
   Its hallowed influence shall around be shed.

IN MEMORY OF H. G.

Oh! if a wish could bring him, teach thy heart
    To school itself to patience; life has snares:
Insidious dangers from time's wayside start,
    And where the wheat was sown spring up the tares.

Happier by far that in the early spring
    Of life's young freshness he should be recalled,
E'en though o'er thee his early transit fling
    Such shadow as the bravest has appalled.

His earthly race was run. What was there here
    But thy kind voice, loved mother, that could stay
His footsteps upward? to a higher sphere
    He passed serenely on, from earth away.

Be thou resigned; a mission still is thine
    To toil awhile upon this weary road;
Tasks are upon thee from a Hand Divine,
    Pointing thee upward to the throne of God.

HARRIET.

She left us in her early prime,
   While flowers of life were round her here;
Yet not until the hand of time
   Had made the loveliest dry and sear.

Her lot was cast 'mid light and shade,
   Her clouds of life had rims of gold;
A gift of music for her made
   A wealth of happiness untold.

We loved her for her gentle worth,
   And for her song-inspiring powers,
For the free gush of jocund mirth
   Spontaneous in her happier hours.

We miss her; but we would not hold
   Her back to this our chequered way;
We yield her to a better fold,
   A happier home, a brighter day.

MAXIMS.

Bind not thy conscience with a vexing vow.
The Future is contingent; guard the Now.

Of the *little* sins beware;
Guard the lips with jealous care.
If the tongue's rebellious still,
Curb it with an iron will.

Let motives be well understood;
Adopt not wrong and call it good.
If evil tempt with hope of gain,
See that thy self-respect remain.

Whatever wrongs thy heart endure,
Keep thy own conscience spotless, pure.

When pettish words arise within thy mind
  And rush for utterance to the willing tongue,
Smooth down thy *tones* till they are soft, refined,
  And fret not others whom perchance they 've stung.

www.ingramcontent.com/pod-product-compliance
Lightning Source LLC
Chambersburg PA
CBHW020730100426
42735CB00038B/1534